Early Settlement

By Dianne Irving

Pearson Australia
(a division of Pearson Australia Group Pty Ltd)
707 Collins Street, Melbourne, Victoria 3008
PO Box 23360, Melbourne, Victoria 8012
www.pearson.com.au

First published 2014 by Pearson Australia
2018 2017 2016
10 9 8 7 6 5 4 3 2

Publisher: Dian Faulisi
Project Managers: Tamara Pirois and Rachel Davis
Editor: Johanna Rohan
Cover & Series Designer: Jenny Grigg
Designer: Nina Heryanto
Copyright & Pictures Editor: Katy Murenu
Mac Operator: Rob Curulli
Illustrator: Fiona Lee
Printed in Australia by the SOS Print - Media Group

ISBN 978 1 4860 0766 0
Pearson Australia Group Pty Ltd ABN 40 004 245 943

Acknowledgements
We would like to thank the following for permission to reproduce copyright material.
The following abbreviations are used in this list: t = top, b = bottom, l = left, r = right, c = centre.
AAP: Mark Graham, p. 22.
Alamy Ltd: Mary Evans Picture Library, p. 15; Karl Johaentges, p. 19.
Corbis Australia Pty Ltd: Cannon Collection, p. 17.
Mitchell Library, State Library of NSW: Francis Wheatley, Captain Arthur Phillip, 1786, a928087, p. 6; a189003, p. 21; a128112, p. 5.
Museum Victoria: NU 33139, p. 9.
National Library of Australia: p. 14.
Pearson Asset Library: Richard Hook © Dorling Kindersley, p. 10.
Powerhouse Museum: p. 13.
Shutterstock: pp. 1, 3, 4, 7, 10tr, 13bl, 15cr, 20, back cover.

Every effort has been made to trace and acknowledge copyright. However, should any infringement have occurred, the publishers tender their apologies and invite copyright owners to contact them.

Disclaimer
Some of the images used in *Early Settlement* might have associations with deceased Indigenous Australians.
Please be aware that these images might cause sadness or distress in Aboriginal or Torres Strait Islander communities.

Contents

Great southern land 4

The voyage 6

Life aboard 10

The new settlement 14

Aboriginal people 18

Connections 22

Glossary 23

Index 24

Great southern land

In 1770, the east coast of Australia was explored by Captain James Cook. He claimed this land for England, and named it New South Wales. The **botanist** Joseph Banks was on the same voyage. He named an area they sailed past Botany Bay. He thought it would be a great place for a new **settlement**.

Years later in 1787, England began to send **convicts** to New South Wales. This was because there were not enough jobs in England, so there was lots of crime and the jails were full. The convicts, along with other passengers, were sent on a fleet of 11 ships. This fleet was called the First Fleet. The new settlement at Botany Bay was the start of European settlement in Australia.

Did you know?
The word 'Australia' comes from the Latin word *australis* meaning 'southern'.

LET'S FIND OUT

- **Who was aboard the First Fleet?**
- **How were the convicts treated?**
- **What problems did the new settlers face?**
- **How did European settlement impact Aboriginal people?**
- **Why do people come to Australia today?**

Captain Phillip raising the British flag

The voyage

In 1787, the First Fleet left England and set sail for Australia. The 24 000 kilometre voyage would take the fleet eight months and they would stop three times.

Captain Arthur Phillip was in command of all the 11 ships in the First Fleet.

13 May 1787

The First Fleet left Portsmouth early on a Sunday morning. There were around 1 500 passengers on board the 11 ships. They included convicts, **officers**, **marines**, women and children.

The First Fleet included:

- Two naval ships – *Sirius* and *Supply*
- Six convict ships – *Alexander*, *Charlotte*, *Friendship*, *Lady Penrhyn*, *Prince of Wales* and *Scarborough*
- Three **store-ships** – *Borrowdale*, *Fishburn* and *Golden Grove*.

Did you know?

The *Lady Penrhyn* was the only convict ship carrying female convicts. There were around 101 female convicts on board. The ship was also carrying horses. They were to become the first horses in Australia.

3 June 1787

The fleet's first stop was at Tenerife, in the Canary Islands, off the north-west coast of Africa. They stayed here for one week. While they were here, fresh food and water were loaded on board the ships to replace the stocks they had used. The fleet left on 10 June.

5 August 1787

The fleet's next stop was Rio de Janeiro, in Brazil. They stayed here for one month. During this time, the ships were cleaned and repaired, plants and seeds were collected to take to the new settlement, and everyone was treated to the local food. The fleet left on 4 September.

13 October 1787

The fleet's third stop was Cape Town, in South Africa. Again, they stayed for one month. They collected more plants and seeds to take to the new settlement. They also collected lots of animals – four horses, seven cows, two bulls, four goats, 44 sheep, 32 pigs, and lots of **poultry**. The fleet left on 12 November.

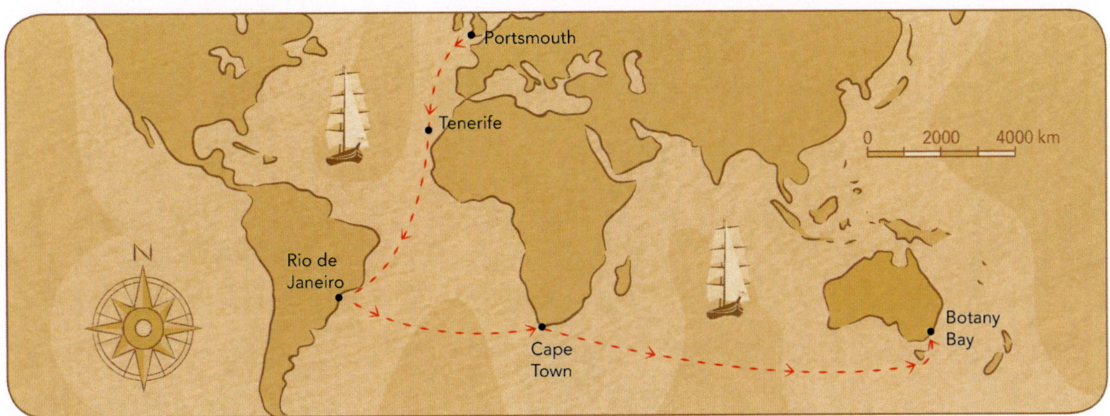

A map of the First Fleet's route showing stops along the way.

18–20 January 1788

After eight months at sea, the First Fleet reached Botany Bay. The *Supply* was the first ship in the fleet to arrive on 18 January. The other 10 ships in the fleet arrived on 19 and 20 January. It was quickly decided that Botany Bay was not a good place for a settlement. There was not enough fresh water, and the soil was too poor to grow crops.

21 January 1788

Captain Phillip decided to look for a better place for the settlement. A group set out and searched north of Botany Bay. They found a bay that was perfect – Port Jackson. It was sheltered, and had lots of fresh water. It also had fertile soil. They returned to Botany Bay on 23 January.

13 May
First Fleet leaves Portsmouth, England for Australia.

5 August
The fleet stops in Rio de Janeiro, Brazil for one month to make repairs and get new supplies.

1787 ← May June July August September October

3 June
First Fleet stops at Tenerife, in the Canary Islands, off the coast of Africa.

13 October
First Fleet stops in Cape Town, South Africa, for one month.

25 January 1788

Captain Phillip and his ship left Botany Bay and sailed to Port Jackson. The other 10 ships left Botany Bay the next morning.

26 January 1788

By nightfall, all the ships in the fleet had arrived at Port Jackson. They dropped anchor close to the shore. Captain Phillip named this spot Sydney Cove after Lord Sydney, who had helped organise the voyage.

This coin from 1938 shows the British flag being raised at Sydney Cove on 26 January, 1788.

18 January
First Fleet reaches Botany Bay. The first ship to arrive was the *Supply*.

25 January
Captain Phillip and his ship sail to Port Jackson.

1788

November December January February March April 1788

21 January
A group sets out and finds a better place for a settlement, Port Jackson. The decision is made to settle here.

26 January
The other 10 ships arrive at Port Jackson.

Life aboard

The exact number of people that sailed on the First Fleet is not known. However, it is thought there were around 1500 people aboard the 11 ships. During the voyage, around 22 babies were born and around 48 people died.

The crew

The fleet had around 320 officers and crew, and each ship had a captain in command. Captain Arthur Phillip was captain of the *Sirius*, as well as being in charge of the whole fleet. There were around 250 marines on board, some travelling with their wives and children. The marines were sent to guard the convicts and keep the peace in the new settlement.

The other passengers on board included a judge, a surgeon and his assistants, a **chaplain**, and an official in charge of the ships' supplies.

This painting shows British officers guarding a group of convicts.

Convicts

The number of convicts aboard the First Fleet is thought to be around 775 – with 582 men and 193 women. Nearly all the convicts were from England and Ireland. However, there were some who had come to England from America, France, China and Africa. Most of the convicts were between 20 and 40 years old. The oldest convict was 68 years old, and the youngest convict was only 13 years old!

Many convicts had been found guilty of theft. They had stolen items such as clothes, rope, bread and money. Around 250 of the convicts had originally been sentenced to death for their crimes. But, their sentences were changed to **transportation** to Australia. The lengths of their sentences were seven years, 14 years or life.

Did you know?

Coins engraved with messages or transportation details were often given to loved ones by convicts before they left England.

Aboard!

Who?	How many?
officers, crew	320
marines	250
convicts	775
others	155
Total	**1 500**

The conditions

Convicts were kept in crowded and dirty conditions on the prison deck below the main deck. However, the convicts of the First Fleet were treated well compared to convicts transported to other places around the world. Captain Phillip allowed them time above deck for fresh air and exercise. He also made sure they were not punished too harshly, and that they had fresh food, when it was available.

The convicts were locked up behind bars, and some were kept in chains.

Diseases

The most common diseases on board were **dysentery** and **scurvy**. Around 48 people died during the voyage. This was a very low number for such a journey at this time. On the **Second Fleet**, two years later, about 278 people died on board only six ships.

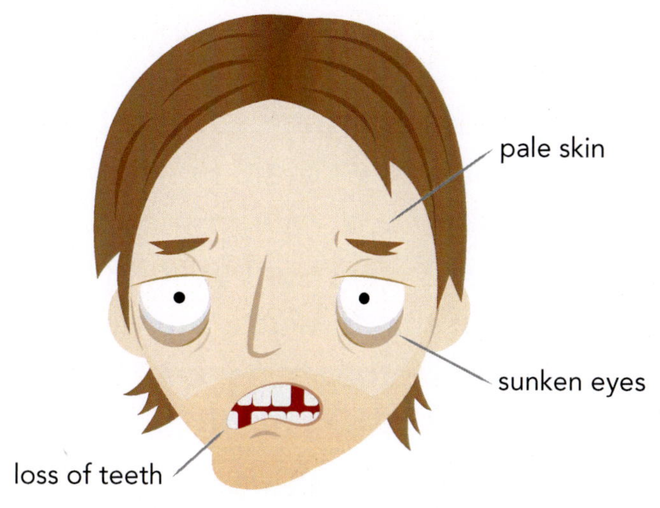

Common symptoms of scurvy

The supplies

The store-ships had to bring enough supplies to last for two years in the new settlement. They brought tools and building materials such as saws, wheelbarrows, bricks and nails. They brought tents, so people had shelter while they built huts and other buildings. They also brought cooking **utensils**, clothes and beds.

Seeds and plants were also brought to the new settlement so people could grow their own food. During the voyage, more seeds and plants, along with animals were collected.

Plants on board the First Fleet included strawberry, banana, orange, prickly pear and Spanish reed.

The new settlement

Shortly after the First Fleet arrived at Sydney Cove, tents were pitched so Captain Phillip, and certain officers and marines were able to stay on shore. The next day, some of the male convicts were sent ashore. Over the next days and weeks, the rest of the convicts, marines, women, children and animals were all brought ashore. Everyone was put to work – buildings needed to be constructed, land needed clearing, and crops needed planting.

An early engraving of the Sydney Cove settlement, 1788. The eleven ships of the First Fleet are depicted anchored in the harbour. Buildings, camps, work areas and gardens are also shown.

Hardships

The settlers faced many hardships. The trees were much harder to cut down than they expected. Therefore, it took longer to build the huts and other buildings they needed. Many of the crops that were planted died or were eaten by **native** animals. Food was scarce and the settlers were put on **rations**. And, new supplies they needed from England did not arrive.

The convicts

The convicts were made to work and given jobs to match their skills. They worked as brickmakers, farmers, nurses and servants. Some convicts were placed in charge of other convict workers. Unskilled convicts were put to work building roads.

Convicts who disobeyed orders were whipped, or put in **leg-irons**. Those who committed a crime, such as stealing food, could be punished by death.

Convicts with no special skills were made to build roads. This was called 'hard labour'.

There were some convicts who tried to escape. A group walked back to Botany Bay, where they saw a fleet of French ships. They asked the French if they could work on the ships. The French said no, and the convicts were forced to return to the settlement. Other convicts tried to survive in the bush, but they failed because they couldn't find enough food. And, a few escaped convicts thought they could easily walk north to China!

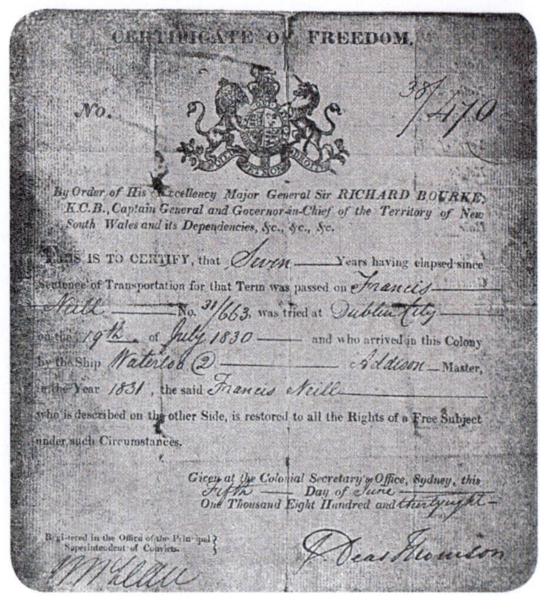

CERTIFICATE OF FREEDOM.

No. 38/470

By Order of His Excellency Major General Sir RICHARD BOURKE, K.C.B., Captain General and Governor-in-Chief of the Territory of New South Wales and its Dependencies, &c., &c., &c.

THIS IS TO CERTIFY, that Seven Years having elapsed since Sentence of Transportation for that Term was passed on Francis Neill No. 31/663 was tried at Dublin City on the 19th of July 1830 and who arrived in this Colony by the Ship Waterloo (2) Addison Master, in the Year 1831, the said Francis Neill who is described on the other Side, is restored to all the Rights of a Free Subject under such Circumstances.

Given at the Colonial Secretary's Office, Sydney, this Fifth Day of June One Thousand Eight Hundred and thirty eight

Registered in the Office of the Principal Superintendent of Convicts.

This ticket-of-leave says the convict Francis Neill is free after finishing a seven-year sentence.

Over time, many of the convicts were freed. They had either finished their sentences, or they were **pardoned**. Some stayed in Australia and lived their lives as free settlers, working and earning a living. Others decided to return to England.

More people arrive

In 1790, the Second Fleet of convicts arrived in Sydney Cove, followed by the Third Fleet in 1791. Convicts began to be sent to other parts of Australia, such as Van Diemen's Land (Tasmania), Port Macquarie and Moreton Bay. In 1793, the first group of free settlers arrived at Sydney Cove. The settlement was now much larger, and other parts of New South Wales began to be settled.

Transportation ends

Convict transportation to Australia ended in 1868. The last convicts transported from England were sent to Western Australia – to where Perth is today.

Did you know?

In 1868, the population of the new settlement of Australia had reached about 1.5 million people.

From the First Fleet until this time, 806 ships had brought around 165 000 convicts to Australia.

Circular Quay, Sydney, 1868

Aboriginal People

The Aboriginal and Torres Strait Islander Peoples have lived in Australia for thousands of years. At the time of the first European settlement, Aboriginal people lived as hunters and collectors, gathering their food from the land and in the sea around them.

There were many different Aboriginal groups, each with their own language, **customs** and laws. These groups belonged to a special area of land. They cared for this land, protected this land and made sure they did nothing to harm it.

Did you know?
There were more than 250 languages spoken by the Aboriginal people, before the arrival of the European settlers.

The impact of European settlement

The settlers and the Aboriginal people had very different ways of living. They spoke different languages making **communication** between them difficult. They also treated the land in very different ways. Both groups had trouble explaining their differences, and their worries, to each other.

Sometimes, both groups were friendly to each other. The Aboriginal people would invite the settlers to join them in a corroboree. A corroboree is a special ceremony with singing and dancing. Other times, the Aboriginal people and the settlers did not get along.

An Aboriginal rock painting in Arnhem Land, Northern Territory, shows British ships arriving in Australia.

The problems

European settlers took over large areas of land, clearing it for farming and building houses on it. This meant that the Aboriginal people lost land they depended upon for their living.

The settlers also hunted the same animals and fish as the Aboriginal people. Food became harder for the Aboriginal people to find. All these things led to fighting between the two groups, and people from both groups were killed.

The name 'wallaby' comes from the Eora people, who were the first inhabitants of the Sydney area.

Diseases

Many Aboriginal people died from diseases the settlers brought into Australia. One of the most deadly diseases was **smallpox** – it killed many Aboriginal people.

Due to European settlement, many Aboriginal groups were forced to move to their different areas. Over time, it became more and more difficult for Aboriginal people to continue their traditional ways of life.

Did you know?

Other diseases that spread from the settlers to the Aboriginal people were chickenpox, influenza and the measles.

A pencil drawing from 1875 showing Aboriginal people and European settlers

Connections

Today, people choose to come to Australia from many countries around the world. People are no longer forced to, like the convicts were during early European settlement.

People come to Australia for many different reasons. Some people come to work. Other people come because it is less crowded than their own country. Then there are some people who come because it is safer than where they lived before.

Most of the settlers in the First Fleet were from England and Ireland. Today, people from countries all around the world call Australia home. These people have brought with them different customs and traditions, making modern-day Australia, a very **multicultural** country.

These people are new Australian citizens. They are at an Australia Day citizenship ceremony, in Canberra.

Glossary

botanist someone who studies plants

chaplain a person who leads religious services

communication the giving of information

convicts people found guilty of a crime

customs traditional ways of doing things

dysentery a disease causing very bad diarrhoea

leg-irons chains placed around the ankles

marines soldiers who work on ships

multicultural made of many different cultures

native belonging to a particular place

officers people in charge

pardoned excused from a crime

poultry domestic birds, such as chickens

rations things shared out in a fixed amount

scurvy a disease caused by a lack of vitamin C

Second Fleet the second group of ships sent to New South Wales from England

settlement a place newly set up; also known as a colony

smallpox a deadly disease causing fever and a skin rash

store-ships ships used to carry supplies

transportation the sending of convicts to another country to live as prisoners

utensils tools used for cooking or eating

Index

A
Aboriginal people 18, 20, 21

B
Banks, Joseph 4
Botany Bay 4, 8, 9, 16

C
Cape Town 7, 8
convicts 4, 6, 10, 11, 12, 14, 15, 16, 17, 22
Cook, Captain James 4
crimes 4, 11, 15
customs 18, 22

D
disease 13, 20

E
England 4, 6, 8, 11, 15, 16, 22

F
First Fleet 4, 6, 8, 10, 11, 12, 14, 17, 22

I
immigrate 22

L
Lord Sydney 9

M
marines 6, 10, 11, 14
multicultural 22

N
New South Wales 4, 16

O
officers 6, 10, 11, 14

P
pardoned 16
Phillip, Captain Arthur 6, 8, 9, 10, 12, 14
Port Jackson 8, 9
Portsmouth 6

R
rations 15
Rio de Janeiro 7

S
scurvy 13
Second Fleet 13, 16
settlement 4, 7, 8, 9, 10, 13, 14, 15, 16, 17, 18, 20, 22
ships 4, 6, 7, 8, 9, 10, 13, 16, 17
smallpox 20
supplies 8, 10, 13, 15
Sydney Cove 9, 14, 16

T
Tenerife 7
transported 12, 17

V
voyage 4, 6, 9, 10, 13